A PLAN FOR THE PEOPLE

NELSON MANDELA'S HOPE FOR HIS NATION

WRITTEN BY
LINDSEY McDIVITT

ILLUSTRATED BY
CHARLY PALMER

EERDMANS BOOKS FOR YOUNG READERS

GRAND RAPIDS, MICHIGAN

President Nelson Mandela had white hair, kind eyes, and a wide, warm smile. But many times over his long life he'd had no reason to smile. Many times his eyes had glittered with anger at injustice. Many times he'd come close to giving up hope for change in his country—South Africa.

Nelson Mandela had hope for his own bright future back in his early years.

He had hope while growing up in his Xhosa village—roaming free on the grasslands like Black princes before him. Men who led South Africa before White men arrived.

He had hope while attending the University of Fort Hare,
the only college for Blacks in a country governed by Whites.
Mandela was hot-headed at times, but hard-working.

He had hope
while relishing
life in the big city,
Johannesburg, where he
first made White friends.
Mandela started out poor,
but kept learning. Soon
he worked as a lawyer,
sported sharp suits,
and drove a fancy
American car.

But South Africans with dark skin were ruled by those with white skin. Often Mandela was treated as less than a man—called "boy" by White people. Anger blazed in Nelson Mandela like a grass fire in the African bushveld.

Then new laws caged his people. Blacks required permission to live, work, even visit in White areas. They were squeezed into the poorest parts of the nation. Or pushed into sad, rickety shacks on the edges of cities.

The White government created categories to divide all South Africans by race or color—Black, White, Indian, or "Colored" (people of mixed race). Separation of the races, apartheid, became the heartbreaking law of the land. Even married couples—one Black, one White—could no longer stay together. Separate buses, beaches, even benches. Separate schools—where Black people were trained only to serve Whites.

As a lawyer, Mandela defended dark-skinned South Africans against unjust White laws. He wanted freedom not just for himself, but for all of his people.

Vowing to strike down the laws of apartheid, Mandela joined the African National Congress. A natural leader, he drew people in—like wildlife to water in the dry Karoo.

The ANC and other groups of Black South Africans demanded changes to the harsh laws. There were many ways to fight for freedom. They marched in the streets after curfew. They boarded Whites-only train cars. They defied the rules and burned the passbooks they were required to carry.

Believing in a nation for all races, some White, Indian, and mixed-race South Africans joined with the ANC in creating a plan, one that Mandela now embraced. One that would make everyone equal citizens, respected and with the right to vote.

In 1955, their Freedom Charter proclaimed: "We, the people of South Africa, declare for all our country and the world to know: that South Africa belongs to all who live in it, black and white . . . "

But the powerful White government used deadly bullets against unarmed protesters, and hope for peaceful change was crushed. Some freedom fighters felt forced to try other tactics. Trying hard to avoid harm to people, they attacked government targets like telephone poles and power plants.

Fearing Mandela and his fellow activists would take over, the government arrested them and put them on trial.

Nelson Mandela, Ahmed Kathrada, Raymond Mhlaba, Elias Motsoaledi, Walter Sisulu, Andrew Mlangeni, Govan Mbeki. Banished to tiny Robben Island—for life.

"WE STAND BY OUR LEADERS"

Clank. Cold. Alone.

Mandela, now prisoner 466/64, was in a cell so small his head and feet could touch the walls. He slept there on the floor. He ate there. He exercised there an hour each morning.

He ached to see his wife and five children. Daughters Zindzi and Zenani, so small. No visits allowed for children under sixteen.

The first year—only one visitor, one time. Winnie, his wife. Twenty-one years would crawl by before he was allowed to even touch her hand.

In the beginning, just two letters sent and two received each year. Rules tore even love letters to tatters.

No mention of the struggle against apartheid.

No mention of another prisoner or their family.

No newspapers.

Just across the bay, but a world away—Cape Town glittered. It was there, more than three hundred years ago, that ships brought the first White people to South Africa. Now White guards marched Mandela and the other prisoners to the quarry to chop stone.

How to stay freedom fighters?

Behind bars the struggle for equal rights for dark-skinned South Africans continued. But they would need to fight in different ways.

Mandela covered fear with confidence. Courage.
And calm.

With the ANC's vision in mind—a nation for all South
Africans—he set aside his bitterness and anger at
White South Africans. He even encouraged prisoners
to befriend their prison guards. Mandela realized
racism itself was the enemy.

Mandela and his friends readied themselves to be
the leaders their nation needed. This required news
from the world outside prison. Sneaking newspapers
from the trash heap when guards looked away, they
shared all the information they could. Whispered
across locked cells. Written in invisible ink made
with milk. Delivered in tiny coded notes.

To the guards, the prisoners looked as lazy as
lions in the shade. But they were sharpening skills,
preparing and planning, mapping a new future for
all South Africans.

Eventually allowed books through the mail, Mandela studied law, politics, religion, history. Education held the key to their cage. With Mandela's encouragement, the older prisoners taught prisoners new to Robben Island. As younger prisoners learned political lessons, and even earned college degrees, Robben Island became known as "The University."

Mandela also urged the young White guards to study. He believed education might free them of the hateful apartheid beliefs they'd been taught. Perhaps one by one they could learn to respect people of all colors.

Early lessons from his elders drifted through Mandela's mind. They'd schooled him in kindness to others. And also in "ubuntu," the African idea of shared humanity—the idea that all people are linked like a delicate spider web.

Nelson Mandela dove deep into the complicated history of his country—a nation rich in resources and a diversity of people. Native San, Khoi, and Bantu-speaking groups were the earliest inhabitants of South Africa. White colonizers came from Europe centuries later, along with the people they brought from other countries to work for them—some enslaved. Many groups and people of all colors now called South Africa home. But those with white skin held all the power and most of the land.

Seeking to understand why some refused to respect those with dark skin, Mandela studied his White guards up close. He learned the language they spoke, Afrikaans, gaining their trust and respect. Talking with them, he watched young minds begin opening to new ideas.

But days dragged, and decades passed. Time was counted in guards' shrill whistles and shouts.

Over the years some rules were relaxed, and small pleasures brightened their days. Milk for morning tea. Music by South African Miriam Makeba, and American Nat King Cole. A fresh peach.

The Black prisoners and White guards wove stories for each other, dipped rusks in hot tea, spoke of family problems—the kind of contact not allowed outside the prison walls.

Mandela grew to understand that all people, Black and White, needed to be set free from the hateful system of apartheid. He realized that "a man who takes away another man's freedom is a prisoner of hatred, he is locked behind the bars of prejudice and narrow-mindedness."

Long, slow years took a toll. Mandela grieved when a mother chameleon in his garden abandoned six tiny babies. He longed for his own struggling family.

His small garden soothed him. What did he grow? Chilies, tomatoes, and onions to spice up dull prison food. He shared with his jailers.

Other things grew too—respect and an understanding of how Mandela and his friends wished to change South Africa was growing in the minds of some guards. When leaving the island, a hard warden wished the prisoners good luck. Another guard broke the rules and placed Mandela's new granddaughter in his arms. Just for a moment. A baby. It had been so long.

Meanwhile, efforts to gain Mandela's freedom were growing around the world. The government hoped he'd be forgotten. No words or pictures of Mandela were allowed. In South Africa, news, books, movies, and even music were all censored.

But the African National Congress made Mandela the symbol of their struggle. His voice echoed through time, words spoken at his trial: "During my lifetime I have dedicated myself to this struggle of the African people. I have fought against white domination, and I have fought against black domination. I have cherished the ideal of a democratic and free society in which all persons live together in harmony and with equal opportunities."

Nelson Mandela stood tall, but still behind bars. Thousands of cards arrived for his 60th birthday. Just six reached his hands. The rest were burned.

South Africa burned too. Pressure from people outside the country, and those within—even some White citizens—made it impossible for officials to govern.

Mandela secretly reached out to government officials, and amazingly they brought him to talk in Cape Town. Perhaps Mandela could guide this troubled country to peace? He surprised them by speaking Afrikaans. He shocked them with knowledge of their history. He astounded them by understanding the needs and fears of all South Africans.

Finally, at age 71, after decades of hard work and struggle, Mandela walked free.

He held out hope, but Blacks boiled with anger. He held out forgiveness, but Whites trembled with fear. The world watched and prayed that they would find a peaceful path forward.

A true leader, Mandela stayed calm. Careful. Controlled. Defusing violence demanded all the skills he'd learned over twenty-seven years in prison.

When finally presidential elections opened to citizens of all races, Mandela voted with other Black South Africans for the first time. "Nkosi Sikelel'iAfrika! God Bless Africa!"

Elected President, Mandela formed a new multiracial government, including friends from Robben Island. He even pulled in one prison guard to work alongside them. His people were free, but there was so much work to do toward equality.

People of all colors sent ideas for a new Constitution to preserve their fresh freedoms. South Africa's Bill of Rights showed off—a shining new example of democracy.

After five years he stepped down to allow South Africa's young democracy to function, but his work for the health and welfare of his people continued. Those made poor by apartheid still had many needs, including work, housing, health care, and better schools.

To many in South Africa, he was Madiba, an honored elder.

To others, Tata, beloved Father of a new country.

To the world, he was a hero. Gifts galore showered down. The Nobel Peace Prize—a huge honor.

But a most treasured present arrived from a child. A note from a White South African girl—Wilma Verwoerd, just thirteen.

When Mandela went to prison, her great-grandfather was South Africa's leader. The man who designed apartheid, to keep Black and White apart.

"You've changed my life for the better. You've taught me to love people of all races and colors."

—Wilma Verwoerd

Can you picture Mandela's wide smile?

Another step away from fear and prejudice.

Another step in the fight for freedom
from racism.

Another step in the journey toward
South Africa as "one nation, one people."

Change was sweeping his beloved country,
South Africa.

AUTHOR'S NOTE

I was born in the same land as Nelson Mandela, but growing up in the United States during the time when apartheid laws ruled South Africa, I wasn't proud of my South African heritage. My family had been part of the White minority that suppressed the rights of the Black majority in South Africa. We traveled there from the U.S. every three years to visit my grandparents. During those trips I saw signs requiring that Blacks use separate benches from Whites, even separate doorways into the post office. Grown-up Black people were called "boy" or "girl" by Whites. As a child, I was puzzled. As a teen, I was angry and confused. As I matured, Black suffering in South Africa became more obvious. I felt guilt, sorrow, and hopelessness. Like my parents, I became convinced the nation could never change peacefully. We feared for family left behind.

We wrestled with loving our country, South Africa, after recognizing the lies of its police-state propaganda. The only differences between its people were inflicted by apartheid—poverty, poor education, and broken families. It became harder to look away from hateful policies that hurt innocent human beings. But there was sadly little discussion of White supremacy in our small Minnesota town. Or in our family—as we felt shame for our heritage.

I embraced America and became a citizen. I tried to find my way forward—to recognize racism, and stereotypes of all kinds, to call them out. I worked hard to raise open-minded children. Discussing discrimination became easier after choosing schools with students of all colors. I learned that educating myself about racism is a lifelong process.

Twenty-five years went by before I revisited South Africa—this time weeks after Nelson Mandela's death. Evidence of that nation's love for Madiba colored Cape Town, and people of all races mourned. Change had come to South Africa—true progress toward the Freedom Charter's 1955 plan. A plan I'd just learned of, fifty years later. As the tour boat left Cape Town for Robben Island, I reflected that Mandela was imprisoned in 1962—the year I immigrated to America as a small child. He was still in prison during my 1989 visit, to introduce my baby son to my grandmother.

How could I explain to my son and daughter—now decidedly anti-racist young adults—that some of our family once believed their white skin made them better than others? We were descended from French Huguenots who had fled religious persecution to the tip of Africa in 1689. From European colonists who benefitted enormously from White privilege. From family who looked away from the pain inflicted by apartheid.

But our family also included an Afrikaner politician who fought fiercely for the voting rights of Black South Africans, and helped establish Fort Hare University. It included family arrested for protesting apartheid, and others who broke the law to shelter Black activists. Family who embraced the new democratic South Africa.

On Robben Island, I peered into Nelson Mandela's prison cell, filled with questions. How did he know that White people behaving hatefully could change? How did he bring all South Africans together? He brought peace to a country with a violent history, and birthed a brand new democracy. This book was born from my search for answers. I learned that Mandela believed race should not divide people in any way. He prepared himself in prison to lead South Africans of all colors.

"No one is born hating another person because of the color of his skin," Mandela said. "People must learn to hate, and if they can learn to hate, they can be taught to love, for love comes more naturally to the human heart than its opposite." This story seemed important to share.

South Africa still struggles with vast inequality between races. But it's an amazing nation—trying to lead the way against all odds. Today around the world White people are being challenged to change. We created racist policies hundreds of years ago, then racist ideas to justify them. Now we must fight racism with all we've got. We can change, one person at a time. We can be brave and educate ourselves. Dig deep to bring racist beliefs out of the shadows. Speak up—with our voices and our pens. Let's work hard, really hard, at loving and respecting each other. Let's honor Nelson Mandela's plan for the people.

— LINDSEY McDIVITT

ILLUSTRATOR'S NOTE

Illustrating *A Plan for the People* was a natural next step after illustrating *Mama Africa!*, about anti-apartheid activist Miriam Makeba. I could carry over so much research from that project into this one. But long before either book, I had painted a portrait of Mandela, just for myself, and collected several books about him. I would also like to thank my lovely wife Karida for introducing me to South Africa, which we now consider our second home. In Johannesburg we visited the Apartheid Museum, which only grew my love and respect for Mandela.

As I sketched and painted, I also relied on Lindsey's notes about my interpretations. My first sketch of Mandela's cell showed him wearing long pants. But Lindsey pointed out that, for Mandela's early years on Robben Island, Black prisoners were only issued short trousers. They had to fight for the right to wear long pants! From prison cells to the rural landscapes of Mandela's childhood, Lindsey's comments helped ground my paintings in history.

Though *A Plan for the People* addresses serious topics, I had no desire to make my illustrations too intense. I wanted to convey the spirit I've experienced in South Africa, a Mandela-like spirit of love and forgiveness. So I stayed true to a palette of warm, bright colors, and I consistently incorporated the bold patterns worn by the people and tribes of South Africa. These almost-abstract patterns helped me tie my work to a consistent theme.

As an artist, my ongoing challenge is not to overthink or overwork. I have to remember to stop and see what happens. I usually create an official sketch, then fill in the color. But I painted the ending portrait of Mandela in a way that I never paint anything: I started with those warm, bright colors and then brought the detail into it. Sometimes— like a jazz musician weaving in and out of the beat—you need to step out of the way and let what happens happen.

In South Africa today—even years after Madiba's death—I can still see the impact of his strength, pride, confidence, and love. Nelson Mandela spent decades in prison for his beliefs, and he still came out with a loving spirit for his people. That fact inspires me, and I try to instill that lesson in my children: it's not about you. It's about something so much bigger. How can you further not only yourself but those that are around you?

Everywhere you go, you'll run into people disillusioned with politics and activists. But I believe that President Mandela was sincere and genuine in his desires for his people. We are often in the presence of greatness, and we're not even aware of it. Our elders may be traumatized by their experiences, or they may dismiss their stories as not being relevant or important. But their experiences have helped us to be where we are. We're always standing on the shoulders of giants—giants like Nelson Mandela.

— CHARLY PALMER

A BRIEF HISTORY OF APARTHEID

The Republic of South Africa is a country located at the tip of Africa. European people colonized the area beginning with the Dutch in the seventeenth century—calling themselves Afrikaners. Colonists developed racist ideas that Whites were better than darker-skinned people there. A cruel, complicated set of laws was created by a White government in the twentieth century to separate the races and control Blacks, who far outnumbered Whites. This system became known as "apartheid" [a-PART-tate], meaning "separateness."

Starting around 1910, specific segregation policies took away Blacks' job security and rights to own land, travel, or live where they wanted. During World War II many moved to cities, and White supremacist beliefs grew stronger from Nazi influence. In 1948 the National Party (which advocated for apartheid) took control of the government. Although Blacks had no voting rights, and only a minority of White voters actually voted for that party, the National Party's policies shaped everyone's lives for forty years.

From 1948 to the 1980s, every part of life was controlled by laws enforcing separation of the races and legalizing separate-but-not-equal facilities. Over the years the security police gained more power than the courts. People of all races were persecuted and jailed for breaking apartheid laws or speaking out against them. Censorship meant that books, movies, and other media could be banned, and personal mail could be examined and confiscated.

MAJOR EVENTS RELATED TO APARTHEID IN SOUTH AFRICA

1949 — The Prohibition of Mixed Marriages Act meant Whites and people of other races could not be married to each other.

1950 — Population Registration Act classified all residents as "White," "Colored" (mixed race), or "Native" (Black), later called Bantu. All people were issued identity cards listing their race. ("Indians" or "Asians" were only recognized as permanent residents in 1959.)

1950 — The Group Areas Act allowed the government to decide who could live in any part of the country. They could remove people using force.

1950 — The Suppression of Communism Act outlawed the Communist Party, but was used to silence anyone criticizing the government.

1951 — The Bantu Authorities Act forced Blacks into poor rural areas—"tribal reserves"—falsely called their true "homelands."

1953 — The Reservation of Separate Amenities Act separated public facilities such as toilets, benches, and beaches with signs. The Bantu Education Act stated that Blacks should have educational facilities separate from Whites. Because these facilities were not equal, Black citizens could purposely be kept in jobs serving White citizens.

1960 — On March 21, 1960, police shot and killed sixty-nine unarmed Blacks protesting apartheid laws. Over 180 were injured. This became known as the Sharpeville Massacre.

THE ANC STRUGGLE AGAINST APARTHEID

By the early 1950s, Nelson Mandela was convinced all races must work toward a nation for all—that racism was the enemy. Whites had been in South Africa so long that they had nowhere to go, but they needed to change. This was ANC policy— but not all groups working for change agreed.

In 1955 the Congress of the People adopted the Freedom Charter, envisioning a South Africa with equal rights for people of all colors. Thousands of volunteers had recorded people's demands—such as better education, and better working and living conditions. It was a powerful tool in the struggle.

There were a small number of Whites fighting apartheid, but the government labeled anyone fighting apartheid a communist and terrorist. Fear of communism meant the ANC lost the support of Britain and the United States early in the struggle.

Mandela admired the nonviolent civil rights strategies of Martin Luther King Jr. and Mohandas Gandhi. But in South Africa, Blacks were not considered citizens and had no protections. For years freedom fighters fought apartheid peacefully, but the government responded with harsher laws and violence.

Following the Sharpeville Massacre, the ANC formed a branch called Umkhonto we Sizwe (the Spear of the Nation) in 1961, focused on destroying government targets like telephone poles, railway lines, and pass offices. They wanted to avoid harming people—hoping all races might have good relations in a new South Africa. Mandela looked for support in London and throughout Africa.

While Mandela was in prison, many people gave up their lives in the struggle. Other nations withheld money and support to encourage the government to change. Violent unrest made it difficult to govern. Some White South Africans joined the struggle for change. Mandela secretly reached out to the government to talk. Between 1985 and 1989, while still in prison, he met with government officials including President Botha and President de Klerk. The government was finally realizing that the system of apartheid needed to end.

MANDELA'S PRISON TIME

Nelson Mandela and his fellow activists were imprisoned together first at Robben Island. Because political prisoners were separated by race, Denis Goldberg, a White activist, was kept at a different prison in solitary confinement for 22 years. Often the wardens were brutal, and early conditions were degrading, including hard labor. Black Africans were given no socks and only short pants—to remind them they were "boys." Privileges such as university correspondence courses were only granted after pressure from international organizations and particularly from Helen Suzman, long South Africa's lone member of Parliament fighting apartheid. Letters were severely limited and always heavily censored. Being imprisoned together did give Mandela and the others an opportunity to secretly make plans and share the vision of the ANC with other prisoners.

During Mandela's imprisonment, his wife Winnie was herself often interrogated and imprisoned. It was a struggle to support their family. Mandela did have feelings of anger and bitterness at the great suffering of his family. But he believed that showing anger decreased his power. Mandela believed prison helped him change himself for the better, crediting the support and determination of his friends. But prison broke many others, and he felt great empathy for them. Nelson Mandela served twenty-seven years in prison (Robben Island, Pollsmoor Prison, and finally Victor Verster).

The prisoners discussed "nonracialism" for years. Mandela would not discriminate against Whites in the goal to end discrimination. Their aim was to gain the trust of the government and lead a nonracial nation. ANC policy was to try and educate all people, and the prisoners succeeded in changing some prison guards.

TIMELINE OF MAJOR EVENTS IN NELSON MANDELA'S LIFE AND SOUTH AFRICA'S JOURNEY TO DEMOCRACY

1652   The Dutch East India Company establishes a settlement at the Cape of Good Hope to provide fresh supplies to ships rounding the tip of Africa.

1795   First British occupation of the Cape.

1910   After fighting two bitter wars (known as the Boer wars) for control of South Africa's land and resources, British and Afrikaner colonists unite to form the Union of South Africa.

1912   The South African Native National Congress (SANNC) is founded with the goal of fighting for the rights of Black South Africans. In 1923 it was renamed the African National Congress (ANC).

1918   Rolihlahla Mandela is born on July 18 at Mvezo, Transkei, South Africa. A teacher later gives him the name "Nelson."

1939   Mandela enrolls at University College of Fort Hare. In 1940 he is expelled for joining a student protest.

1941–1943   Mandela works in Johannesburg and finishes a Bachelor of Arts degree via correspondence studies at University of South Africa. He begins attending ANC meetings.

1944   Mandela co-founds the ANC Youth League. He marries Evelyn Ntoko Mase, and they have four children together.

1949   South Africa's National Party begins passing apartheid laws.

1952   With Oliver Tambo, Mandela opens South Africa's first Black law firm. The ANC begins the Defiance Campaign, a series of peaceful protests against apartheid.

1955   The Congress of the People—the ANC along with White, Black, Indian, and "Colored" allies—draws up the Freedom Charter.

1956   Mandela and 155 other anti-apartheid activists are charged with treason. A four-year court case begins. Mandela and the others are found not guilty in 1961.

1958   Mandela and Evelyn divorce. He marries Nomzamo Winnie Madikizela, and they have two daughters together—Zenani and Zindzi. Hendrik Verwoerd becomes Prime Minister.

1960   The government bans the ANC and similar anti-apartheid groups.

1962   Mandela travels throughout Africa seeking advice and is arrested upon his return. He is sentenced to five years in prison for leaving the country illegally and inciting unrest.

1963   The "Rivonia Trial" begins. Mandela faces counts of sabotage and knows the death penalty is possible.

1964   Before sentencing, Mandela speaks for four hours—his famous "I Am Prepared to Die" speech. Along with seven others, he is found guilty and sentenced to life in prison.

1968–1969   Mandela's mother, Nosekeni Fanny, dies soon after visiting him on Robben Island. Mandela also learns that his son Thembekile has died in a car accident. He is not allowed to attend their funerals.

1980	Winnie Mandela visits Robben Island with their infant granddaughter Zaziwe. Prison guard Christo Brand breaks the rules, allowing Mandela to briefly hold Zaziwe.
1980–1981	Over 200,000 people sign the "Free Mandela" petition.
1986	The United States Congress approves the Comprehensive Anti-Apartheid Act, joining many other countries in imposing strict economic and cultural sanctions on South Africa.
1989	From prison, Mandela completes his LLB Bachelor of Law degree from the University of South Africa.
1990	On February 2, the ANC is unbanned. On February 11, Mandela is released from prison at age 71.
1990–1991	The four main apartheid laws are repealed.
1992	86% of White South Africans vote on a referendum. 68.7% vote in favor of a new reformed South Africa.
1993	The Interim Constitution grants equal rights to all South Africans. Mandela and President de Klerk jointly receive the Nobel Peace Prize for their work ending apartheid.
1994	On April 27, Mandela votes for the first time in his life. On May 9, he is elected the first president of a fully democratic South Africa.
1996	Nelson and Winnie Mandela divorce. South Africa begins the Truth and Reconciliation Commission hearings on human rights violations committed during apartheid.
1997	A new South African Constitution is adopted. The Bill of Rights—which names the civil, political, economic, and cultural rights of South Africans of all races, genders, sexual orientations, and ages—is one of the most liberal in the world.
1998	On his eightieth birthday, Mandela marries Graça Machel.
1999	Mandela steps down as president and establishes the Nelson Mandela Foundation.
2010	Mandela makes his final public appearance at the FIFA soccer World Cup in Johannesburg.
2013	Mandela passes away on December 5. His memorial service is one of the world's largest-ever gatherings of international leaders, with about 170 countries represented.

MORE BOOKS ABOUT MANDELA'S LIFE

Brown, Laaren, and Lenny Hort. *Nelson Mandela: A Photographic Story of a Life*. London: DK, 2006. Juvenile nonfiction.

Cooper, Floyd. *Mandela: From the Life of the South African Statesman*. New York: Puffin, 1996. Picture book.

Fraser, Sean. *The Children's Madiba: The Life Story of Nelson Mandela*. Illus. Tom Kyffin. South Africa: Puffin Books, 2013. Juvenile nonfiction.

Mandela, Zindzi, and Zazi and Ziwelene Mandela. *Grandad Mandela*. Illus. Sean Qualls. London: Frances Lincoln, 2018. Picture book.

Nelson, Kadir. *Nelson Mandela*. New York: Katherine Tegen Books, 2013. Picture book.

Nelson Mandela Foundation with Umlando Wezithombe. *Nelson Mandela: The Authorized Comic Book*. New York: W.W. Norton & Company, 2009. Graphic nonfiction.

Van Wyk, Chris, adapt. *Nelson Mandela: Long Walk to Freedom*. Illus. Paddy Bouma. New York: Roaring Brook, 2009. Picture book.

MORE BOOKS ABOUT MANDELA'S WORLD

Bildner, Phil. *The Soccer Fence: A Story of Friendship, Hope, and Apartheid in South Africa*. Illus. Jesse Joshua Watson. New York: G.P. Putnam's Sons, 2014. Picture book.

Erskine, Kathryn. *Mama Africa!: How Miriam Makeba Spread Hope with Her Song*. Illus. Charly Palmer. New York: Farrar, Straus and Giroux, 2017. Picture book.

Sisulu, Elinor Batezat. *The Day Gogo Went to Vote*. Illus. Sharon Wilson. New York: Little, Brown, 1999. Picture book.

Tutu, Archbishop Desmond and Douglas Carlton Adams. *Desmond and the Very Mean Word*. Illus. A.G. Ford. Somerville, Mass.: Candlewick, 2012. Picture book.

Wright, Adrienne. *Hector: A Boy, a Protest, and the Photograph that Changed Apartheid*. Salem, Mass.: Page Street Kids, 2019. Picture book.

WEBSITES AND VIDEOS TO EXPLORE

"Nelson Mandela Foundation: Living the Legacy." The Nelson Mandela Foundation, 2020. nelsonmandela.org.

The Nelson Mandela Foundation's website hosts extensive archives, digital exhibitions, and information on inequality-fighting initiatives in South Africa today.

"Nelson Mandela." C-SPAN, 2020. c-span.org/person/?nelsonmandela.

The network offers dozens of free videos of Mandela's speeches and appearances, including his 1990 speech as the first Black private citizen to address the United States Congress.

Peralta, Eyder. "Listen: Two Mandela Speeches that Made History." NPR, 6 December 2013. npr.org/sections/thetwo-way/2013/12/06/249210908/listen-two-mandela-speeches-that-made-history.

This article features clips of some of Mandela's most famous speeches: his 1964 "I Am Prepared to Die" speech at the Rivonia Trial and his 1994 address at his presidential inauguration.

"Robben Island Prison Tour." Robben Island Museum, 2020. artsandculture.google.com/exhibit/robben-island-prison-tour-robben-island-museum/mQIim-e6wopSJw?hl=en.

Designated as a World Heritage Site in 1999, Robben Island is now a museum and nature conservation area. This website provides a virtual tour of the island guided by former political prisoner Vusumsi Mcongo.

SELECTED BIBLIOGRAPHY

Cohen, David Elliot, and John D. Battersby. *Nelson Mandela: A Life in Photographs*. New York: Sterling, 2009. Print.

Brand, Christo, with Barbara Jones. *Mandela: My Prisoner, My Friend*. New York: Thomas Dunne Books-St. Martin's Press, 2014. Print.

Clark, Nancy L. and William H. Worger. *South Africa: The Rise and Fall of Apartheid*. 2nd ed. Harlow, England: Longman, 2011. Print.

Kathrada, Ahmed. *Letters from Robben Island, a Selection of Ahmed Kathrada's Prison Correspondence, 1964-1989*. 2nd ed. Ed. Robert Vassen. Cape Town: Zebra Press, 2000. Print.

Maharaj, Mac, et al. *Mandela: The Authorized Portrait*. Kansas City, MO: Andrews McMeel, 2006. Print.

Mandela, Nelson R. *Conversations with Myself*. New York: Farrar, Straus and Giroux, 2010. Print.

Mandela, Nelson. *Long Walk to Freedom: The Autobiography of Nelson Mandela*. New York: Little, Brown and Co., 1994. Print.

A Prisoner in the Garden: Photos, Letters, and notes from Nelson Mandela's 27 years in prison. The Nelson Mandela Foundation. New York: Viking Studio, 2006. Print.

Sampson, Anthony. *Mandela: The Authorized Biography*. New York: Knopf, 1999. Print.

Time Special Commemorative Edition: Nelson Mandela: A Hero's Journey 1918-2013, January 2013. Print.

Waldmeir, Patti. *Anatomy of a Miracle: The End of Apartheid and the Birth of the New South Africa*. New Brunswick, New Jersey: Rutgers University Press, 1997. Print.

Dedicated to the people of South Africa
and the United States—all colors, doing the hard work
toward true democracy and equality for those
with dark skin. As Nelson Mandela once said,
"there are many more hills to climb."

— L. McD.

Dedicated to Rev. Joseph Lowery,
Congressman John Lewis,
and Rev. C. T. Vivian;
and all the freedom and justice fighters to come . . .

— C. P.

SOURCES

"We, the people of South Africa, declare…" Congress of the People, Preamble to the Freedom Charter, qtd. in *South Africa: The Rise and Fall of Apartheid* (London: Routledge, 2016), pp. 134-137.

"A man who takes away . . . " Mandela, Nelson, *Long Walk to Freedom* (New York: Back Bay Books, 1995), p. 624.

"During my lifetime I have dedicated myself . . . " Mandela speech at Rivonia Trial, qtd. in Sampson, Anthony, *Mandela: The Authorized Biography* (New York: Random House, 1999), p. 192.

"You've changed my life . . . " Note from Wilma Verwoerd, *Time Special Commemorative Edition: Nelson Mandela: A Hero's Journey 1918-2013*, January 2013, p. 120.

" . . . one nation, one people . . . " Mandela, Nelson, *Long Walk to Freedom* (New York: Back Bay Books, 1995), p. 620.

"No one is born hating another person . . . " Ibid., p. 622.

". . . there are many more hills to climb." Mandela, Nelson, *Long Walk to Freedom* (New York: Back Bay Books, 1995), p. 625.

Text © 2021 Lindsey McDivitt
Illustrations © 2021 Charly Palmer

Published in 2021 by Eerdmans Books for Young Readers,
an imprint of Wm. B. Eerdmans Publishing Co.
Grand Rapids, Michigan
www.eerdmans.com/youngreaders

29 28 27 26 25 24 23 22 21   1 2 3 4 5 6 7 8 9

Library of Congress Cataloging-in-Publication Data

Names: McDivitt, Lindsey, 1957- author. | Palmer, Charly, illustrator.
Title: A plan for the people : Nelson Mandela's hope for his nation / written by Lindsey McDivitt ; illustrated by Charly Palmer.
Description: Grand Rapids, Michigan : Eerdmans Books for Young Readers, 2021. | Audience: Ages 7+ | Summary: "This biography follows Nelson Mandela from his work with the African National Congress, to his imprisonment on Robben Island, to his extraordinary rise to the presidency"— Provided by publisher.
Identifiers: LCCN 2020036588 | ISBN 9780802855022 (hardcover)
Subjects: LCSH: Mandela, Nelson, 1918-2013—Juvenile literature. | Presidents—South Africa—Biography—Juvenile literature. | Anti-apartheid activists—South Africa—Biography—Juvenile literature.
Classification: LCC DT1974 .M42 2021 | DDC 968.071092—dc23
LC record available at https://lccn.loc.gov/2020036588

Illustrations created with acrylic paint.

We are grateful to Dr. Robert Edgar, professor emeritus of African Studies at Howard University, for sharing his expertise.

A percentage of the author's profit from the sale of each book will be donated to the Nelson Mandela Foundation.